The Kids' Solution Workbook

by Lawrence E. Shapiro, Ph.D.

The Center for Applied Psychology, Inc.
King of Prussia, Pennsylvania

The Kids' Solution Workbook
by Lawrence E. Shapiro, Ph.D.

Published by:
The Center for Applied Psychology, Inc.
P.O. Box 61587, King of Prussia, PA 19406 U.S.A.
Telephone: 1-800-962-1141

The Center for Applied Psychology, Inc. is the publisher of Childswork/Childsplay, a catalog of products for mental health professionals, teachers, and parents who wish to help children with their social and emotional growth.

Printed in the United States of America.

ISBN 1-882732-62-6

Part 1: Solution Activities for Parents & Teachers

Part 2: Solution Activities for Kids

Introduction

Over the last five years, Solution-Oriented Therapy has become an increasingly popular approach to dealing with a wide variety of problems. Based to a large extent on a systems approach to therapy (i.e., looking at the context of the problem rather than just the individual who has the problem), Solution-Oriented Therapy has become so popular so quickly because of its accessibility and simplicity.

In fact, simplicity is one of the basic tenets of this approach. This form of therapy avoids jargon and diagnostic labeling and favors finding simple solutions even to complex problems. Steve de Shazer, Ph.D. (1984) sums up the basic premises behind this form of therapy through a metaphor. Dr. de Shazer explains that although people with problems often seek help because they feel that they are inadequate or incompetent, this is really only a misperception. He notes that in fact these same people solve complicated problems every day, and they are probably very competent in other areas of their lives. For some reason, however, they cannot apply these same skills to the problem at hand. De Shazer explains that they actually have the solutions to their problems, but it is as if they are behind a locked door and don't have the key. If they can just find the right key, they will be able to open the door and utilize solutions that have worked for them before. It is usually the job of the counselor or therapist to help people find just the right key, and it is the intent of this book to aid in that process.

The first part of this book consists of exercises for parents and teachers and other adults in the child's life. It is adults who have the true decision-making power, as well as a history of finding solutions, so naturally adults should take the lead in helping a child with his or her problems. It is not important that a concerned adult (usually a parent or teacher) do all the exercises in this section or that they approach them in a particular order. Any given exercise may hold the "key" to the door which is keeping a solution away.

The second part of the book consists of exercises for children seven years and older, with each activity based on a principle of Solution-Oriented Therapy. Most of these exercises will require some help from an adult, but they will undoubtedly give children new ways to look at their problems. Adults may also find this section helpful.

There is no wrong way to do any of these activities. They are meant to stimulate new ways to think about the common problems of children and the roles that adults can play in helping them solve these problems. They are designed to be a starting point for helping children and the people who care about them find new solutions to old problems. Open communication and support systems will keep this process going.

Part 1:

Solution Activities for Parents & Teachers

Exercise #1:
Knowing Where to Start

Objective: To identify how to start turning problems into solutions.

Children who are referred for counseling often have multiple problems, but nearly everyone agrees that problems are best solved one at a time. Although some people feel that you should start with the hardest or most serious problem first, this really doesn't make sense from a psychological point of view. Instead, we will start with the problem that is most easily solved, with the understanding that success leads to more success.

Make a list of the problems that you observe in the child about which you are concerned. List up to 10 problems. Then rank them according to the degree of difficulty in solving the problem, with 1= most readily solved and 10= most difficult to solve.

Child's Name: _____	Date: _____

Rank	Problems You Are Concerned About

Exercise #2:
Thinking in Terms of Solutions

Objective: To start thinking in terms of solutions.

The most important thing to remember in finding solutions is to keep things simple. Many people expect too much of themselves (and others) and miss the obvious answers to their problems.

Take the first two problems on your list from Exercise #1 and think of as many solutions for them as possible. Think of 100 if you can! This is a brainstorming exercise, so it doesn't matter whether the solutions are realistic or not. The important thing is to keep generating solutions. If you have difficulty with this, get several other people to help you brainstorm ideas. Usually more ideas come up in a group of people working towards a common goal.

After writing down every idea, go back and circle the ideas that are feasible.

Then go back a third time and prioritize the solutions that you circled, ranking them from easiest to most difficult. Try the easiest one first. Don't think of reasons why it *won't* work...think of reasons why it *will* work!

Child's Name: _____ **Date:** _____

First **Ranked Problem:** _____

Solution Ideas

Rank	Idea

Child's Name: _____ **Date:** _____

***Second* Ranked Problem:** _____

Solution Ideas

Rank	Idea
_____	_____
_____	_____
_____	_____
_____	_____
_____	_____
_____	_____
_____	_____
_____	_____
_____	_____
_____	_____
_____	_____
_____	_____
_____	_____

Exercise #3:
Communicating Solutions

Objective: To start talking in solution-oriented terms.

One of the most important ways to start changing problems into solutions is to start talking about new possibilities and directions. Some of the worst things you can do is to put labels on people or look for and dwell on negative things about the child. *When you communicate in solution-oriented language, you will be more likely to see solutions to the problem.*

Child's Name: _____ **Date:** _____

A. Try this exercise in changing negative ways of thinking and communicating them as positive ones.

Describe the child's problem in compassionate rather than pathological terms (e.g., Pathological = "He has ADHD." Compassionate = "He has a problem in self-control.").

Think of a time when you complained about the child to someone else. Write exactly what you said. Then, under it, write something you could have said which would open up the possibility of a solution, rather than scapegoating the child.

Write what you said that would be considered a pathological term:

_____

_____

_____

_____

_____

_____

Write what you could have said instead, in more compassionate terms:

_____

_____

_____

_____

B. Write five things that you could say to the child you are concerned about to help him understand that he has choices, without blaming him or making him feel bad.

For example: "It is very hard for me to talk when you interrupt, *but I know you have something important to say. You could say it when I'm finished, or you could write it down and say it later when we have a time where you do all the talking. Which would you prefer?*"

1. _____

_____

2. _____

_____

3. _____

_____

4. _____

_____

5. _____

_____

C. Write five negative adjectives that you commonly use to describe the child you are concerned about. Then write the opposite of these adjectives and just one small thing that the child could do to earn this positive description.

For example: Negative adjective: *inconsiderate*
Positive adjective: *considerate*
What can be done: *He could carry in the groceries from the car without being asked.*

Now try and have him or her do these five things in one day.

1. Negative adjective: _____

Positive adjective: _____

What can be done: _____

_____

_____

2. Negative adjective: _____

Positive adjective: _____

What can be done: _____

_____

_____

3. Negative adjective: _____

Positive adjective: _____

What can be done: _____

_____

_____

4. Negative adjective: _____

Positive adjective: _____

What can be done: _____

_____

_____

5. Negative adjective: _____

Positive adjective: _____

What can be done: _____

_____

_____

Exercise #4:
Combining Solutions

Objective: To see how one solution can lead to another.

Once you start thinking in terms of solutions rather than problems, you will start to see how one solution can relate to more than one problem. For example, Mary's parents were concerned about her always being very uncooperative and difficult at home and at school. They decided to work on a small piece of the problem, to make her easier to be with. They implemented a program using the philosophy of Random Acts of Kindness and required her to do one kind thing each day. This made it easier for her parents, her teachers, her siblings, and her friends to be with her. One simple solution addressed many problems.

Think of a simple thing that you can ask the child you are concerned about to do, that addresses several aspects of her problem or several different problems. Stretch your imagination. Think of many ways that one solution could change many things.

Child's Name: _____ **Date:** _____

One Simple Change Asked of Child: _____

_____

_____

Potential Areas and/or People Who Could Be Affected:

_____

_____

_____

_____

_____

_____

Exercise #5:
Taking the First Step in
Solving the Problem

Objective: To see how one solution can have a "ripple effect" and solve other problems as well.

A central idea behind solution-oriented thinking is that problems are related and solving one small problem will effect other positive changes. It is like throwing a pebble in a pond; there is a ripple effect that spreads out from the center in all directions.

Imagine that when you take the first step to solving a problem it spreads out and affects many other people and situations. Write the first change that you will make in the center circle, and then write in the people or situations that might be affected (even in a small way) by your change.

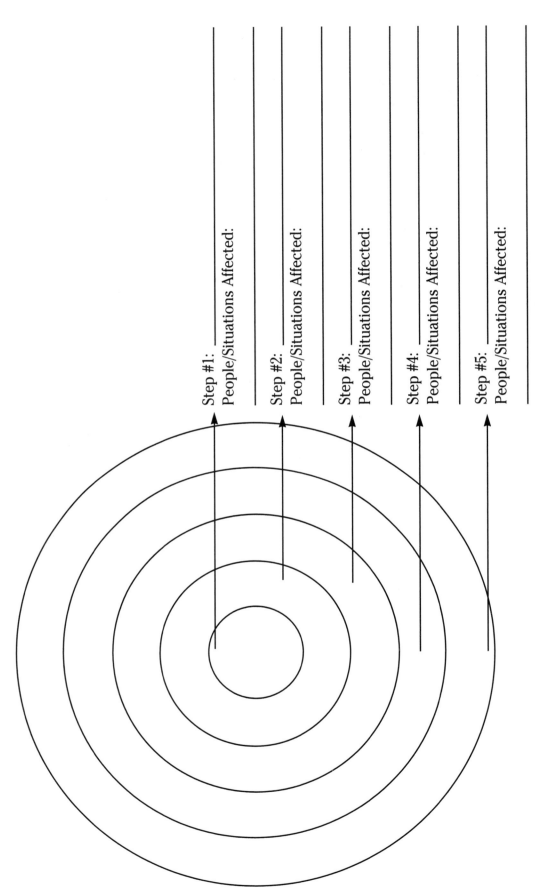

Step #1: _____
People/Situations Affected: _____

Step #2: _____
People/Situations Affected: _____

Step #3: _____
People/Situations Affected: _____

Step #4: _____
People/Situations Affected: _____

Step #5: _____
People/Situations Affected: _____

Exercise #6:
Looking at Problems Others Have Solved

Objective: Finding solutions from the example of others.

Problems tend to isolate people. It seems to be in our human nature (or at least in our culture) to think that we must bear a problem alone or that no one else has had this problem before. Obviously neither of these thoughts are true.

Think of three people you know who have found solutions for similar problems. For example, one family had a child with a serious health problem. Their neighbor had a child with chronic asthma who was now grown, and they were able to talk about their trials and successes.

Be a little unconventional when looking for solutions. They may not be obvious. *Remember that people find solutions to very serious problems every day! You can, too.*

Identify three people who have had a problem somewhat similar to the one you are having now with your child or your student. Write their names below along with the problem as you understand it. Then call them on the phone and ask them what they did. Be open and candid. Write down anything that might help you with your current concern.

1. Person: _____

His/Her Problem: _____

_____

_____

What You Learned: _____

_____

_____

_____

2. Person: _____

His/Her Problem: _____

_____

_____

What You Learned: _____

_____

_____

_____

3. Person: _____

His/Her Problem: _____

_____

_____

What You Learned: _____

_____

_____

_____

Exercise #7:
Finding People Who Are Part of the Solution

Objective: Finding people who can help in your solutions.

As mentioned in the previous exercise, people tend to isolate themselves with their problems, and this tends to make the problem worse. Learn to rely on other people to help you with a problem that you are having with your child/student. *Remember, you are not in this alone.*

Write the names of 10 people who can help, even in a very small way. Don't be shy about asking for help. Wouldn't you do the same for someone else?

Child's Name: _____   **Date:** _____

Problem You Are Having with the Child: _____

_____

1. Person: _____

_____

The Way He/She Can Help: _____

_____

_____

When He/She Can Help: _____

_____

_____

2. Person: _____

_____

The Way He/She Can Help: _____

_____

_____

When He/She Can Help: _____

_____

_____

3. Person: _____

_____

The Way He/She Can Help: _____

_____

_____

When He/She Can Help: _____

_____

_____

4. Person: _____

_____

The Way He/She Can Help: _____

_____

_____

When He/She Can Help: _____

_____

_____

5. Person: _____

_____

The Way He/She Can Help: _____

_____

_____

When He/She Can Help: _____

_____

_____

6. Person: _____

_____

The Way He/She Can Help: _____

_____

_____

When He/She Can Help: _____

_____

_____

7. Person: _____

_____

The Way He/She Can Help: _____

_____

_____

When He/She Can Help: _____

_____

_____

8. Person: _____

_____

The Way He/She Can Help: _____

_____

_____

When He/She Can Help: _____

_____

_____

9. Person: _____

_____

The Way He/She Can Help: _____

_____

_____

When He/She Can Help: _____

_____

_____

10. Person: _____

_____

The Way He/She Can Help: _____

_____

_____

When He/She Can Help: _____

_____

_____

Exercise #8:
Creating a Solution Network

Objective: To form a network of people who can help with the problem at hand.

Many cultures stress the role of family and community in solving problems. But for many reasons, this seems to be the exception rather than the rule for most Americans. However, you can create a network to help you with a problem. A network could include traditional self-help groups, on-line support groups, church groups, or community groups that are formed to solve a particular problem. People frequently respond positively to solution-oriented groups once they are formed, but you may have to take the initiative in forming one.

For example, suppose you had a child who was underperforming in school. She just didn't seem to care, and nothing you did seemed to help. *Assume that there are people who have children with similar problems. Assume that people will want to help you if you just ask.*

To find people with a common problem, you could: 1) ask the principal of your school for advice, 2) do a search on the Internet or an on-line service (you can do this at most local libraries if you don't have a computer), 3) speak to a community leader or member of the clergy, and so on. To form a network for yourself or your child/student, you could take the information from Exercise #7 and ask three or four people to make commitments to help in your quest for solutions.

On the next page, list 10 things you can do to help form a solution-oriented network of people who can help you or the child about whom you are concerned. Remember that a support network takes a little time to solidify, but once it does, you will find your life both easier and richer.

Creating a Solution Network

Child's Name: _____

Date: _____

What You Can Do	Short-Term Result	Long-Term Result
1.		
2.		
3.		
4.		
5.		
6.		
7.		
8.		
9.		
10.		

Exercise #9:
Solution Rituals

Objective: To start doing rituals that anticipate a solution.

Rituals are activities people do without thinking, and yet these rituals are extremely important to them. For example, you might check all the windows and doors in the house before you go to sleep. Or you might have a bedtime ritual with your child, where you sing her a song or tell her a story each night. Rituals usually are comforting because they have a practical purpose and a higher meaning as well. Telling a story to your child undoubtedly helps her relax in order to get to sleep, but it also conveys the message of your love and caring.

Suppose you made up a ritual that would help solve the problem about which you are concerned. What might it be? Let's say, for example, you had a child who wet his bed. You would certainly have him go to the bathroom just before bedtime, but you might also have him practice getting out of bed to go the bathroom during the night. Perhaps each night, he would get in bed and under the covers, but then get up, walk to the bathroom, try to urinate, and go back to bed. He would do this three times. This ritual would convey to him the importance of getting up by himself and might actually help him do it. Positive rituals can become positive habits.

Now think of a ritual that you could teach your child/student that might provide part of a solution to the current problem. Don't make it too hard. It should be easy enough so that it can become a habit almost without effort.

Solution Rituals

Child's Name: _____ **Date:** _____

Describe Problem: _____

_____

_____

Steps of Ritual	Behavior/Action
1. _____	_____
2. _____	_____
3. _____	_____
4. _____	_____
5. _____	_____
6. _____	_____
7. _____	_____
8. _____	_____
9. _____	_____
10. _____	_____

Message Sent/Received by Your Child or Student: _____

_____

_____

_____

_____

Exercise #10:
Thinking in Small Steps

Objective: To start thinking in terms of small steps to a solution.

Problems are best solved in small steps. When you think in small steps, even problems that seem to be insurmountable can be solved. For example, adolescents who are severely mentally handicapped have been taught to make their own beds by breaking the task down into 250 small steps! Each step is learned one at a time and then combined with the other steps. But with patience, the whole task can be learned and the person can make the bed with minimal supervision.

Think of a goal for the child/student about whom you are concerned. Now write 20 small steps to get to that goal. When you make the steps or subgoals very small, they are much easier to attain.

Child's Name: _____ **Date:** _____

Goal: _____

Thinking in Small Steps

	Subtask	Criteria for Success
Step #1	_____	_____
Step #2	_____	_____
Step #3	_____	_____
Step #4	_____	_____
Step #5	_____	_____
Step #6	_____	_____
Step #7	_____	_____
Step #8	_____	_____
Step #9	_____	_____
Step #10	_____	_____
Step #11	_____	_____
Step #12	_____	_____
Step #13	_____	_____
Step #14	_____	_____
Step #15	_____	_____
Step #16	_____	_____
Step #17	_____	_____
Step #18	_____	_____
Step #19	_____	_____
Step #20	_____	_____

Exercise #11:
Anticipating Success

Objective: To start anticipating what life will be like when the problem is gone.

Psychologists have long recognized the ability that people have to unconsciously create their future. Without thinking about it, they put themselves in situations or make decisions based on needs or conflicts of which they are not really aware. Some people define "neurotic behavior" as behavior that makes things worse for themselves or for others even though this is not their desire.

Recognizing the importance of our unconscious wishes and needs, Solution-Oriented Therapy asks people to concentrate on how things will be in a future where the problem has less influence or may be absent all together. Concentrating on the positive aspects of our lives, rather than on a problem, directs our unconscious to make decisions that will be more productive and beneficial. The term "self-fulfilling prophecy" is a very real psychological phenomenon. You can make your future better or worse—why not make it better?

A. Imagine that the problem that now confounds you is gone in six months or a year. Write about how your life has changed for the better. Be very specific. Be positive, but also be realistic.

_____

_____

_____

_____

_____

_____

_____

_____

_____

_____

_____

_____

B. Now imagine how things will be different for the child about whom you are concerned. Simply project your imagination forward, again for six months or a year, and envision a day in the life of the child, without the present problem. Write about the image that you see.

Child's Name: _____ **Date:** _____

_____

_____

_____

_____

_____

_____

_____

_____

_____

_____

_____

_____

_____

_____

_____

C. Now reread what you wrote in the previous two paragraphs. Does anything come to mind that will make either of these scenes happen? Even if it isn't directly related to the problem, write it down. Tear out this exercise (or make a copy of it) and read it frequently, perhaps once a week. Keep reading about the future. Convince yourself that it can happen. Keep writing even the simplest of ways to make positive changes in your life or the life of the child about whom you are concerned.

Things to Do Differently to Make Positive Changes in My Life:

1. _____

2. _____

3. _____

4. _____

5. _____

6. _____

7. _____

8. _____

9. _____

10. _____

Things to Do Differently to Make Positive Changes in _____ **Life:**

(Child's Name)

1. _____

2. _____

3. _____

4. _____

5. _____

6. _____

7. _____

8. _____

9. _____

10. _____

Exercise #12:
Optimistic Thinking

Objective: To become realistically optimistic regarding the problem about which you are concerned.

Having a positive attitude really does make a difference. Studies have shown optimistic people are less likely to be depressed, perform better at work, and are even physically healthier. Being optimistic is more than just an attitude—it is a way of explaining the world. Optimists see the world realistically. They see bad events as single occurrences, rather than bad luck or fate. They believe that over time, problems work themselves out. They also take responsibility for their actions, knowing when to hold themselves accountable for decisions and when other people are in control of events.

Pessimists distort the way they think. They overgeneralize (e.g., "I always have the worst luck"); they personalize events (e.g., "Everyone is against me"); and they exaggerate negative occurrences (e.g., "This is the worst day of my life!").

Many studies have demonstrated that people can learn to change their pessimistic thinking into more optimistic thinking.

A. Write about a pessimistic way of looking at the worst day you had this month (related to the problem of the child about whom you are concerned).

_____

_____

_____

_____

_____

_____

B. Now write about the same event from the viewpoint of an optimist. Don't be unrealistic. Just be positive in seeing bad things as single events that can be changed and good things as events that can be perpetuated.

_____

_____

_____

_____

_____

_____

Exercise #13:
Solution-Oriented Language

Objective: To use language in a way that encourages solutions.

Speaking and thinking in terms of solutions is an important part of this new approach to solving problems. For example, watch your usage of words that are absolute, like "always," "everyone," or "never." Absolutes are rarely true (notice that I didn't say "never"), and they tend to lead us deeper into the problem, rather than towards a solution. An important part of finding a solution to a problem is finding an exception to the problem.

For example, one teacher complained to a school counselor about a boy who was "always out of his seat." The counselor agreed to observe the boy in order to find a way to solve the problem. But while observing the class for an entire day, the counselor saw that the child was only out of his seat for about two minutes at a time and that this occurred only during transition times, when a new project or activity was being started. The counselor suggested that the teacher have all the children stand up and stretch between activities, and this solved the problem for the boy who was "always out of his seat."

On the following pages, write sentences using the following "absolutes," each one relating to the problem about which you are concerned. Then below each sentence write an exception to the absolute statement. Finally, if you can, write a possible solution that the exception implies.

Define the Problem about Which You Are Concerned:

_____

_____

_____

_____

_____

_____

_____

"ALWAYS"

_____

_____

_____

_____

_____

_____

THE EXCEPTION

_____

_____

_____

_____

_____

A POSSIBLE SOLUTION

_____

_____

_____

_____

_____

"EVERYONE"

_____

_____

_____

_____

_____

THE EXCEPTION

_____

_____

_____

_____

_____

A POSSIBLE SOLUTION

_____

_____

_____

_____

_____

"NEVER"

_____

_____

_____

_____

_____

THE EXCEPTION

_____

_____

_____

_____

_____

A POSSIBLE SOLUTION

_____

_____

_____

_____

_____

"EVERYTHING"

_____

_____

_____

_____

_____

THE EXCEPTION

_____

_____

_____

_____

_____

A POSSIBLE SOLUTION

_____

_____

_____

_____

_____

"CONSTANTLY"

_____

_____

_____

_____

_____

THE EXCEPTION

_____

_____

_____

_____

A POSSIBLE SOLUTION

_____

_____

_____

_____

_____

Exercise #14:
Positive Time

Objective: Building a positive relationship with every child.

When a child has a serious problem, it is common for that problem to completely color his relationships with adults. Whether you are a parent or a teacher, you may come to view the child/student as if he is standing behind a "lens," and that lens is the problem. Without meaning to, you begin to perceive the child in a distorted way, often making the problem worse.

It is important that children have positive time and "problem-free" experiences with the significant adults in their lives. This is an important way to see your child away from the "lens" of his problems. Parents are encouraged to spend some time each day participating with their children in a favorite activity, in a nonjudgmental fashion. Teachers might have one activity a week with a child who is having problems in school, where the child gets to lead the activity, and there is no chance of failure.

Use the form on the next page to plan these positive periods or activities with the child about whom you are concerned. Make sure that the child knows that this is his or her time and you are just there for support. Record what happens and see whether your relationship with the child is improving.

Positive Time

Child's Name: _____ **Date:** _____

Date	Time Period	Activity	Result

Exercise #15:
Positive Discipline

Objective: To plan positive discipline procedures.

Children need love, and they need limits. Most adults have a harder time with setting limits than they do in expressing caring and concern, but discipline is just as important as affection in raising healthy children. There are many effective ways to discipline and/or provide limits for a child, but they need to be thought out before problems occur. Below, write the ways that you plan to handle incidents related to the problem about which you are concerned, as well as ways in which you can handle other types of problems.

Child's Name: _____ **Date:** _____

Behaviors Related to Current Problem	Discipline or Action
_____	_____
_____	_____
_____	_____
_____	_____
_____	_____
_____	_____
_____	_____
_____	_____
_____	_____

Child's Name: _____ **Date:** _____

Other Types of Behaviors That Need to Be Addressed	Discipline or Action
_____	_____
_____	_____
_____	_____
_____	_____
_____	_____
_____	_____
_____	_____
_____	_____
_____	_____
_____	_____

Exercise #16:
Planning Solutions for Yourself

Objective: To see that you are part of any problem and you can be part of any solution.

There is an old saying, "If you are not part of the solution, then you are part of the problem." What do you need to do differently that will help the problem that the child is having—not for the child, but for yourself?

- Do you need to change something about your life so that you are less stressed and more patient?
- Do you need to learn to be more assertive so that you get more of what you need and need less from the child?
- Do you need more support, so that you can give the child/student more support?

Write five things that you need, whether or not they are related directly to the problem about which you are concerned. Then pick two things that you can realistically get for yourself and write how you can get them.

Something You Need	Realistic Need (✓)	How to Get It
1. _____	_____	_____
2. _____	_____	_____
3. _____	_____	_____
4. _____	_____	_____
5. _____	_____	_____

Exercise #17:
Shaping Solutions

Objective: To start shaping behaviors of the child in a desired direction.

Once you have identified possible solutions for the child about whom you are concerned, you can start shaping his or her behavior towards that desired goal. Behavioral shaping is a type of behavior modification to which we are all susceptible. It works. If people keep telling us that we look good when wearing clothes of a certain color, we will start to wear more of that color, without even really being aware that our habits are changing.

The same principle holds true for children. Once you can see beyond the child's problem to new behaviors that indicate the problem no longer exists, you must learn to reinforce those new behaviors. Take, for example, the boy who didn't want to do his homework. Rather than focusing on the problem (his teachers said that he was an "underachiever" and wanted to avoid failure), his parents focused on the solution. They got his teacher to agree to an unusual contract. Their son could either do the homework that was assigned for 1/2 hour per night, or he could do any other learning project for three hours per night. Learning projects included educational videos, computer time, science projects, and so on. The parents praised their son's efforts for whatever he did. Within a short time, he began to do his homework, and he spent time on other educational activities as well.

Write an imaginative solution to the problem that the child about whom you are concerned is having. Make sure that it solves the underlying problem, not just a symptom of the problem. Emphasize new activities or behaviors.

Child's Name: _____ **Date:** _____

The Problem

_____

_____

The Solution

_____

_____

Now rank the best ways to reinforce the new activities or behaviors, with 1 being the best way.

Ways to Reinforce New Behaviors or Activities

_____ Affection

_____ Praise

_____ Token reinforcement

_____ Certificates

_____ Time with the child

_____ Special treats

_____ Special activities

_____ Attention

_____ Other: _____

Exercise #18:
Planning Solution Experiences

Objective: To provide children with experiences that teach them new problem-solving, coping, and social skills.

The main premise behind Solution-Oriented Therapy is that adults can use solutions they learned in the past to solve problems in the present. But children, of course, have a limited storehouse of past solutions to apply to a particular problem, and so we have to make sure that they are given the opportunities to have these experiences.

Experiences should stretch a child into a new area, without being so difficult that they will be frustrating and disappointing. For example, parents of a very defiant child decided that he should spend Saturdays helping out in a nursing home as a way to learn to think about others. But this boy had so little patience or concern about what people thought of him that he found a way to sneak out of the nursing home and was caught stealing candy. A better first experience for him would have been to do chores around the house, where he could be closely supervised.

Think of a variety of experiences that will give the child about whom you are concerned new solutions to present or future problems. Then rate the experiences as to how difficult they may be for the child on a 1 to 10 scale. Put an approximate date as to when you think each activity or experience might happen.

Planning Solution Experiences

Child's Name: _____ **Date:** _____

Experience	Rank	Target Date
_____	_____	_____
_____	_____	_____
_____	_____	_____
_____	_____	_____
_____	_____	_____
_____	_____	_____
_____	_____	_____
_____	_____	_____
_____	_____	_____
_____	_____	_____
_____	_____	_____
_____	_____	_____

Part 2:

Solution Activities for Kids

Exercise #1:
Naming Your Problem

Objective: To think about the problem as "outside" of yourself.

Many children think of themselves as "problem children." Maybe they are too active, or have difficulty in school, or tell lies, and adults seem to always be mad at them. But they aren't the problem...they have a problem. That problem is inside them, and they need to get it outside. It may be running their lives, and it has to stop!

What is the name of your problem? Is it "Charlie?" Is it "The Lying Problem?" Is it "The Sad Monster?"

Giving your problem a name is the first step to getting rid of it. (Who needs it anyway?)

Write three good names for your problem below. Then circle the best one. The best one should make you really hate the problem. Why not? It's causing you trouble, isn't it? It's making people around you upset, isn't it? Choose a name that makes you really mad and will make you want to get rid of your problem as soon as possible.

Name: _____ **Date:** _____

What is your problem? Try to define it.

_____

Now try to come up with three names for the problem and circle the best one.

Name #1: _____

Name #2: _____

Name #3: _____

Exercise #2
What Does Your Problem Look Like?

Objective: To see the problem as different from you.

All right, now that your problem has a name, it needs to look like something. Do you have a hard time controlling your anger? Then I think your problem might be some really nasty-looking monster, with buck teeth and prickly skin. Do you have a hard time talking to new people? Then maybe your problem is a scared little monster that wants you to come and hide in the corner with it. (I wouldn't go if I were you. It's not much fun hiding in the corner.)

Draw your "problem" in the space below. Make it look bad BECAUSE IT IS BAD! YOUR PROBLEM IS MAKING YOU UNHAPPY! WHO NEEDS IT?! GET RID OF IT!

Name: _____ **Date:** _____

Problem's Name: _____

Exercise #3:
A Solution Battle Plan

Objective: To make a plan to fight your problem.

Some people think that to drive out a problem you have to go to battle with it. Maybe this problem has been with you a long time. Maybe it likes living inside you and driving you crazy. Maybe it doesn't want to leave.

BUT YOU CAN DRIVE IT OUT! YOU CAN FIGHT AND WIN! Fill in the Battle Plan below (ask an adult for help if you need it) to help you make a plan to drive your problem out of your life.

Your Personal Battle Plan Against a Problem
That Is Making You (or Others) Miserable

Name: _____ **Date:** _____

Name your enemy: _____

_____

What tools do you need to fight your war? (See the next exercise)

_____

_____

_____

What type of war are you going to fight? Describe different strategies:

Sneak Attack (Come at the problem in a new and tricky way. Surprise is a key element.)

_____

_____

_____

All-Out Battle (Name as many ways as you can think of to attack the problem.)

_____

_____

_____

Guerrilla Warfare (Anything goes!)

_____

_____

_____

Where will the battle be staged?

_____

_____

_____

When is the best time to fight?

_____

_____

_____

Who are your allies? (Who can you trust to help you solve the problem? How are they going to help?)

_____

_____

_____

Designate a problem-free zone (a time and place where you can rest from the fatigue of battle).

_____

_____

_____

Enemies can be sneaky. What do you think your enemy might do to undermine your best plans?

_____

_____

_____

How will you know when the war is won?

_____

_____

_____

What is in your peace treaty? What can you live with and what can't you live with?

_____

_____

_____

What will the future look like now that the war is over?

_____

_____

_____

Exercise #4
Assembling a Tool Kit

Objective: To identify solutions for your tool kit.

Trying to solve a problem can be like fixing a car—you need the right tools. Here are some problem-solving tools that many kids have used to solve problems like yours. Put a check beside the ones that you already use. Circle the ones that you might use in the future.

Problem-Solving Tools

____ Talk to an adult and get advice.

____ Take a deep breath and relax.

____ Take a more positive attitude.

____ Get help from a friend.

____ Find a new behavior that can act as a substitute for the problem.

____ Read a book about the problem.

____ Find someone who has had a similar problem and talk about it.

____ Stick up for your rights.

____ Other _____

Exercise #5:
Learning New Tools

Objective: To think about new ways to solve a problem.

Often when people have a problem, they don't know where to start in solving it. This is true of adults as well as children. Write below what you think your problem is, and then ask everyone you can think of to suggest a solution. Write down each different solution, trying to get as many as you can.

Then rate the solutions as follows:

1 = *bad idea for me*
2 = *maybe this will work*
3 = *I'll try it*

Name: _____	Date: _____
Define Your Problem: _____	

Possible Solution	Suggested By	Solution Rating (1-3)

Exercise #6:
Who's in Control?

Objective: To start taking control of your problem (rather than letting it control you).

Problems are a nuisance. They can really make you miserable. Some people let problems run their lives, and other people see that they can control their problems themselves. Taking control of your problem is the first step to solving it.

For one week, keep a record of who is in control of your life—your problem or you. Mark it on a 10-point scale with:

1 = *The problem is in control*
10 = *I'm in control*

See if you find yourself more in control each day. Why are some days better than others? What can you do to stay in complete control over your own life? Use the space provided to comment on why you think you or the problem had more control that day.

Who's in Control

**The Problem
Is in Control**

I'm in Control

Monday | 1 | | 2 | | 3 | | 4 | | 5 | | 6 | | 7 | | 8 | | 9 | | 10 |

Comments: _____

_____

Tuesday | 1 | | 2 | | 3 | | 4 | | 5 | | 6 | | 7 | | 8 | | 9 | | 10 |

Comments: _____

_____

Wednesday | 1 | | 2 | | 3 | | 4 | | 5 | | 6 | | 7 | | 8 | | 9 | | 10 |

Comments: _____

_____

Thursday | 1 | | 2 | | 3 | | 4 | | 5 | | 6 | | 7 | | 8 | | 9 | | 10 |

Comments: _____

_____

The Problem
Is in Control   **I'm in Control**

Friday | 1 | | 2 | | 3 | | 4 | | 5 | | 6 | | 7 | | 8 | | 9 | | 10 |

Comments: _____

_____

Saturday | 1 | | 2 | | 3 | | 4 | | 5 | | 6 | | 7 | | 8 | | 9 | | 10 |

Comments: _____

_____

Sunday | 1 | | 2 | | 3 | | 4 | | 5 | | 6 | | 7 | | 8 | | 9 | | 10 |

Comments: _____

_____

Exercise #7:
Setting Goals

Objective: To change problems into goals for change.

Some people get stuck on problems rather than finding solutions. It is really all in how you think about it. Changing a problem into a "goal" is a much more positive way to think and will show you a direction in which you can change.

For example, Marty was miserable because everyone picked on her. They said that she had a boy's name and even looked like a boy. Marty would come home from school feeling sad every day. She told her parents that she didn't want to go back to school, but they made her go back anyway. She hated her life.

Then one day, she woke up and decided to stop feeling sorry for herself. She decided to not worry about her "problem" but to think about what she wanted instead. She said to herself, "I'm going to find a friend who accepts me for what I am and who enjoys doing the same kind of things that I do." Immediately Marty started to feel better, because she had a goal.

Can you change your "problem" into a "goal?" Maybe answering these questions will help.

What is something you can work towards that will make you happy?

_____

_____

_____

What is the opposite of your problem?

_____

_____

_____

What is an activity that will help you forget your problem?

_____

_____

_____

What is something that you can do, every day, that will help you with your problem?

_____

_____

_____

What is a goal you could work towards that would make your problem go away, or at least seem less important?

_____

_____

_____

Exercise #8:
Steps to Accomplishing Your Goal

Objective: To see the small steps that will lead up to accomplishing your goal.

Very few goals are accomplished in one step. Usually there are many steps that lead up to accomplishing a goal, and each step brings you closer. For example, suppose you wanted to be a really good basketball player. You would have to practice every day. You would have to try out for a team. You would have to get a good coach or someone to teach you new skills. With every passing day, you would be closer to your goal.

Write the goal that you came up with in Exercise #7. Then list 10 steps to get to that goal. Also write down your target finish date for each step. Remember that the process of getting to the goal is just as important as accomplishing it.

Name: _____ **Date:** _____

Your Goal: _____

_____

Activity	Target Finish Date
_____	_____
_____	_____
_____	_____
_____	_____
_____	_____
_____	_____
_____	_____

Exercise #9:
Concentrating on the Present

Objective: To look for solutions to your problems in the present rather than in the past.

Some people say that every day is like a new page in the book of your life. You can write whatever you like! If you want, you can write today's page as a continuation of your story, or you can start fresh! Suppose that today your story didn't have the same problems as you had yesterday or the day before. Suppose that today you began writing your problem out of your life!

How would you begin to write your problem out of your life? What will today (or tomorrow) look like without having your problem be such an important part?

Try writing about just one day in your life that is a fresh start. Write about a day that doesn't have your problem in it, or at least not very much. Can you make it happen?

Name: _____ **Date:** _____

A Day in My Life

Exercise #10:
Focusing on the Possible

Objective: To see the first place that change is possible.

Sometimes change is easy, and at other times it is difficult. For example, smoking is a difficult habit to change because cigarettes have a drug in them (nicotine) that is addictive. That's why adults are always telling kids not to start smoking, because it is so hard to stop. Other things are easy to change. Wanda's parents were concerned that everyone in the family watched too much TV. So they just put their TV in the closet and only took it out for one hour a night.

When you think about changing a problem that you have, you will see there are many things you could do, many places to start. But some ways to start are easier and some are harder. Write five things you could change right away to help solve a problem you are having. Circle the one that is really easy. Then do it!

Name: _____ **Date:** _____

Define the Problem: _____

_____

Things I Can Change Right Away to Help Solve My Problem

1. _____

2. _____

3. _____

4. _____

5. _____

Exercise #11:
Seeing a Pattern in a Problem

Objective: To start thinking in terms of solutions.

Sometimes things seem really bad. Everything seems to be going wrong. Everything! Then sometimes things start to get better if you see a pattern in your problems. For example, Daryl thought that everyone was always yelling at him. His teacher yelled at him because he was late for school. His dad yelled at him because he missed the school bus. Even his best friend was mad at him because he missed baseball practice. Do you see the pattern in Daryl's problem? Everything had to do with time. He got a watch with an alarm and a day planner, and started using both of them. Then other things started to go right as well.

Is there a pattern to a problem you are having? Think of a problem and write down each part of it. Or write down a series of problems. Is there something that they all have in common? Is there one solution that will affect more than one problem?

Name: _____ **Date:** _____

Problems

1. _____

2. _____

3. _____

4. _____

5. _____

6. _____

7. _____

8. _____

9. _____

10. _____

What, if anything, do the above problems have in common?

_____

_____

_____

_____

Is there one possible solution you can think of to help with most of your problems?
If so, write it below.

_____

_____

_____

_____

Exercise #12:
Understanding That Change Is Constant

Objective: To help see that things will change whether you do anything or not and that this change can help solve problems.

Everything changes. This is particularly true for children, because every day they grow bigger and smarter and learn new things. Whatever problem you have today will be different tomorrow, because you will be different.

Think about how things will change for the problem about which you are concerned. Will change make things easier? If not, why not, and what can you do about it?

Name: _____ **Date:** _____

How will your problem change one month from now?

_____

_____

_____

Six months from now?

_____

_____

_____

A year from now?

_____

_____

_____

Two years from now?

_____

_____

_____

Five years from now?

_____

_____

_____

Ten years from now?

_____

_____

_____

Draw a picture of yourself at the age when the problem has changed even if you did nothing.

Exercise #13:
Changing Things That Keep
the Problem Going

Objective: To identify things that keep the problem from getting better.

Have you ever tried to solve a problem but felt that everything was working against you? Maybe you were right. Maybe there were so many forces keeping the problem going that you just couldn't change it. Kate, for example, had a serious weight problem. She had a hard time running or playing ball, and she often heard other children talking behind her back. She tried to diet, but her parents served fattening foods at every meal. For dinner, they might have fried chicken, mashed potatoes and gravy, all of which Kate loved. Even when Kate used all her willpower and asked for something less fattening to eat, her mom just got mad and said, "This is what I cooked for dinner. Eat this or go hungry." So Kate ate what the rest of her family ate so that her mother wouldn't be mad.

What about the problem you are having? Is there anything or anyone who is keeping the problem from getting better even though he or she doesn't intend to? Be careful before you blame other people for your problems. You must take responsibility for change. But you can also ask for help and point out to others that their behavior affects your problems.

Make a list of people you know well and write down one thing that each person could do to make a problem easier for you to solve. Then ask them if they will do it. If they won't, don't be upset. You simply need to find other people who can help you.

Name: _____

Date: _____

Who Else Can Change to Help You Find a Solution?

Person	How He/She Can Change	Check (✓) if He/She Agrees to Change

Exercise #14:
The Team Approach to Solving
a Problem

Objective: To develop a team approach to finding new solutions.

By now you can see that when it comes to solving problems, few people can do it alone. Things are always easier when you get help from people who care about you. You might say that solving problems is a "team sport." Everyone has a position to play, and you will "win" when everyone plays his position to the best of his ability.

Suppose you could create a team to solve your problem. Who would you put on it? What would each person do? What would you do? Who would be the team captain? Construct your team below, and maybe you will decide to really form the team and get everyone working together!

Name: _____ **Date:** _____

The Team Coach (The person with a lot of skills who trains the others):

_____

The Team Captain (The leader):

_____

The Offensive Players (They actively find new solutions):

_____

_____

_____

_____

_____

The Defensive Players (They guard against attack from things that cause the problem):

_____

_____

_____

_____

_____

The Referee (He or she makes sure that everyone plays by the rules):

_____

_____

_____

_____

_____

REFERENCES

Cade, B. and O'Hanlon, W. H. *A Brief Guide to Brief Therapy*. New York/London: W.W. Norton & Company (1993).

de Shazer, S. *Keys to Solutions in Brief Therapy*. New York/London: W.W. Norton & Company (1984).

Epston, D. and White M. *Narrative Means to Therapeutic Ends*. New York/London: W.W. Norton & Company (1990).

Haley, J. *Problem-Solving Therapy*. New York: Harper & Row (1976).

Metcalf, L. *Counseling Toward Solutions*. West Nyack: The Center for Applied Research Education (1995).

O'Hanlon, W. H. and Weiner-Davis, M. *In Search of Solutions: A New Direction in Psychotherapy*. New York/London: W.W. Norton & Company (1989).